VEGAN
CHEESE

BECOME A 5-STAR CHEESE MAKER

EARNEST CINNAMON

TABLE OF CONTENTS

Introduction 1

Chapter 1: What is Vegan Cheese, and Why Are People going Nuts for it? 3

Chapter 2: Different Types of Vegan Cheese Bases..5

Chapter 3: Equipment and Techniques to get the Best Results! 9

Chapter 4: Easy and Simple Vegan Cheeses & Sauces....................................... 13

Chapter 5: Soft & Fresh Vegan Cheeses 23

Chapter 6: Hard and Air-Dried Vegan Cheeses.. 35

Chapter 7: Fermented and Cultured Vegan Cheeses 47

Chapter 8: Melted Vegan Cheeses 59

Chapter 9: Nut-free Cheeses 65

Chapter 10: How to make the Ultimate Vegan Cheese Board........................ 71

Chapter 11: Keep Your Vegan Cheese Journal... 73

Conclusion.. 75

INTRODUCTION

It's difficult to find great tasting vegan cheeses in the market. So, instead of scouring every supermarket, grocery store, and online store, you should try your hand in making your own!

The best thing about making your own vegan cheese is that you're sure about the ingredients that go in it. You can adjust the taste and volume of the cheeses that you'll make depending on your needs and preferences. It's also a great learning experience if you have a passionate heart for everything vegan.

In this book, you'll find easy recipes as well as challenging ones. There's sure to be a recipe (or two) that you'll love and you'd want to make over and over again.

If you're ready to become a 5-star vegan cheese maker, then this is your chance. Read through the guides and recipes to start creating the best vegan cheeses that you'll ever have!

Thanks for downloading this book, I hope you enjoy it!

CHAPTER 1:

What is Vegan Cheese, and Why Are People going Nuts for it?

You may have seen some vegan cheeses in your local grocery stores and wonder, "Is it possible to make cheese without milk?"

With creative vegans trying to find an alternative to daily food items, countless cheese recipes have been done. There is now a wide selection of dairy-free cheeses in the market and recipes people enjoy.

Vegan cheese is a substitute for the conventional cheese people have grown eating. They're made with non-dairy or plant-based ingredients. Most consumers who buy and eat this type of cheese are vegan, but there are those who simply don't want to consume animal products for health reasons.

Vegan cheeses were first sold commercially in the 1980s. Back then, they weren't as popular as they are now. The first vegan cheeses sold usually tasted bad and had an obvious artificial texture.

Nowadays, vegan cheeses have evolved into something that can compete with commercial dairy cheeses. They taste better and have a texture closer to dairy cheese.

Many vegan cheeses use nuts as a base. They're packed with health benefits and contain fiber, minerals, and probiotics. There are also alternatives for people who have nut allergies. In the next chapter, you'll learn all about your options.

One more thing that attracts people to consume vegan cheese is the wide array of vegan cheese recipes that are easy to do.

If you're ready to make your own vegan cheese at home, continue on to the next chapters.

CHAPTER 2:

Different Types of Vegan Cheese Bases

Before trying any of the recipes in this book, you'll have to know the different bases of vegan cheese. This will help you determine what kind of vegan cheese you can make and enjoy at home.

Here are the ingredients used as a base for vegan cheese:

SEEDS AND NUTS

These are the most commonly used base for homemade vegan cheese.

Seeds and nuts are often soaked, processed, or fermented when used for making dairy-free cheeses. These ingredients taste bland on their own, meaning adding and combining flavors remains easy.

The nuts and seeds most often used for vegan cheese recipes are:
- Cashews
- Macadamia
- Almonds
- Sunflower seeds
- Pumpkin seeds

SOY

Commercial vegan cheeses are commonly soy-based. Soy products are used because they have the closest characteristics to real cheese.

Tofu may be the most widely used form of soy protein for vegan cheese. Both soft or silken and firm tofu can become different types of soft and hard cheeses. Tofu is blander than nuts, so achieving a cheese-like taste is definitely possible.

Soy is sometimes combined with a milk protein called casein. This protein allows the resulting cheese to have a melty characteristic, just like the real thing. But, to be perfectly clear, cheeses with casein aren't considered vegan.

What's a bit worrying though, is that some commercial cheeses labeled as vegan or vegetarian actually contain small amounts of the milk protein.

FLOUR

More often, flour is only a supplementary ingredient to other vegan cheese bases. But, there are some recipes that use flour as the base. Flour is usually used to create vegan cheese sauces though.

Some of the popular starchy flours used for vegan cheese recipes are:
- Tapioca starch/flour
- All-purpose flour
- Potato starch/flour
- Arrowroot flour

VEGETABLES

Some vegan cheeses have root vegetables as the base. The most common vegetables used are carrots and potatoes. Cheeses which use these as bases often have a soft and saucy consistency.

NON-DAIRY MILK

Vegan cheese can also have non-dairy or plant-based milk as a base. It doesn't have casein like animal's milk, so vegan cheeses couldn't mimic the melty quality of real cheese. Other ingredients can be added, however, to somehow make the cruelty-free alternative a bit more similar.

SOLIDIFIED VEGETABLE OILS

One of the things that people love about cheese is the creaminess. Some vegan cheeses use vegetable oils which are naturally loaded with fat, making it possible to copy the creaminess of real cheese. But, oils alone cannot serve as a base. Other ingredients like starch, flour, and agar-agar powder are used to create cheeses with vegetable oils.

CHAPTER 3:

Equipment and Techniques to get the Best Results!

Now that you're ready to start making vegan cheese, let's run through the equipment and techniques you'll need.

BASIC EQUIPMENT

- **A food processor or blender**
  This will be your best friend through your vegan cheese-making journey. It's safe to say that it'll be almost impossible to make most vegan cheese recipes without a blender or a food processor. Try to get a high-powered machine for quick and easy blending or processing.

- **Measuring spoons and cups**
  Making vegan cheese requires accurate measurements. Too much or too little of even just one ingredient can ruin your cheese. Invest in good-quality measuring tools to make the best vegan cheeses.

- **Glass or ceramic bowls**
  You'll be needing a lot of bowls when making vegan cheese. Glass and ceramic bowls are the best to use because they won't affect your cheese's taste and quality. These are important, especially when making fermented or cultured cheese.

- **Non-stick saucepans and pots**

  There will also be a lot of cooking involved when making vegan cheese. Having non-stick pots and saucepans will make everything easier.

- **Silicon scraper**

  Since you'll be using the blender or food processor often, you'll also need a silicon scraper. When blending or processing, many ingredients would be sticking to the sides of the blender or food processor.

- **Mesh strainer or colander**

  These are also important tools, especially when making hard cheeses. You'll need a handy colander or strainer to drain out liquids from your cheese.

- **Cheesecloth**

  Buy quality cheesecloth that has fine holes. Be careful when buying from local grocery stores because they tend to sell low-quality cheesecloth.

- **Airtight storage containers (glass)**

  If you're planning to store your cheeses, you'd have to invest in glass containers which are airtight. These will keep your cheese from spoiling quickly and prevent your home from getting an odd smell.

- **Shaping molds**

  You can use different kinds of molds for your cheese. Get food-grade silicon molds to easily pop out your cheese. You can also use baking pans lined with parchment paper or glass bowls with plastic wrap. Anything will do as long as they're clean.

BASIC TECHNIQUES

There aren't any special techniques needed for making vegan cheese. But, you'll definitely need a steady hand and lots of stamina and patience.

Still, keep in mind that you'll have a lot of mixing and stirring to do. When fermenting or culturing cheese, there are steps where you need to flip your cheese. You need a gentle touch when doing this so your cheese doesn't break or get ruined.

Always keep your hands clean. Any dirt that can contaminate your cheese will ruin the whole recipe.

CHAPTER 4:

Easy and Simple
Vegan Cheeses & Sauces

EASY-AND-SIMPLE VEGAN CHEESE SAUCE

Ingredients:

- 1 tbsp. extra-virgin olive oil
- 1 tbsp. all-purpose flour
- 1 cup cashew or soy milk
- 2 tbsp. nutritional yeast
- A pinch of garlic salt and cayenne pepper powder

Directions:

1. In a small saucepan, heat the oil over medium heat.
2. Add in the flour to the heated oil. Mix well until the flour is dissolved.
3. Slowly add in the milk. Heat the mixture for about 2 minutes or until it slightly thickens.
4. Add the nutritional yeast and a pinch of garlic and cayenne pepper. Mix them all together and let simmer for a few minutes.
5. Transfer the vegan cheese sauce in a glass dish or an uncovered container. Let it cool before serving or you can use it for other recipes.

VEGAN VEGETABLE CHEESE SAUCE

Ingredients:

- 2 pcs. small potatoes, peeled and sliced into ¼-inch pieces
- 1 pc. carrot, peeled and sliced into ¼-inch pieces
- 2 tbsp. nutritional yeast
- 2 tbsp. extra-virgin olive oil
- Half a lemon's juice
- A pinch of garlic salt and cayenne pepper powder
- Minced roasted red peppers, cayenne peppers, or jalapeño (optional)

Directions:

1. Put the potatoes and carrots in a pot. Pour in hot water and cook under low heat.
2. Once the vegetables are cooked, drain the water.
3. Put the cooked vegetables in a blender with all the other ingredients. You can also add in the optional ingredients at this point.
4. Blend all the ingredients together until it's smooth.
5. Transfer the sauce to a serving dish. You can enjoy it with some nachos or steamed broccoli.

EASY NUT-FREE VEGAN CHEESE SAUCE

Ingredients:

- 340 g soft or silken tofu
- ¼ cup nutritional yeast
- ½ cup unsweetened soy milk
- 1 tbsp. white wine vinegar
- 2 tsp. Dijon mustard
- 1 ½ tsp. onion powder
- 1 tsp. salt
- ½ tsp. garlic powder
- ¼ tsp. paprika, smoked

Directions:

1. Combine all the ingredients in a blender. Blend until you get a smooth mixture.
2. Pour the mixture into a saucepan and warm the cheese over low heat. Constantly stir to avoid burning the cheese.
3. Put the heated mixture into a serving bowl and enjoy it with other dishes or treats.

WHITE BEANS VEGAN CHEESE SAUCE

Ingredients:

- 1 cup white beans, cooked
- ½ cup plant-based milk of your choice
- 5 tbsp. nutritional yeast
- ½ tsp. salt
- 1/8 tsp. garlic powder
- ½ tsp apple cider or white vinegar
- 2 tsp. olive oil
- A pinch of dried herbs and spices you prefer (optional)

Directions:

1. Blend all the ingredients in a blender or food processor until smooth.
2. Pour the pureed mixture into a pot over low heat and stir occasionally. You can add more milk if the cheese is too thick for you.
3. Instead of doing Step 2, you can transfer the puree into an instant pot. Set the heat to manual and let it heat up for about 5 minutes.
4. Transfer it to a serving dish or use it for other dishes.

BASIC CASHEW + SWEET POTATO VEGAN CHEESE SAUCE

Ingredients:

- 1 cup raw cashews, soaked for 12 hours
- 1 cup sweet potato, pureed
- ½ cup vegetable broth
- 1 tsp. apple cider vinegar
- ¼ cup nutritional yeast
- ½ tsp. salt

Directions:

1. Put all the ingredients in a blender or food processor. Blend until you get a smooth puree.
2. If the mixture seems too thick, add a bit more vegetable broth. Add in 1 tablespoon at a time until it reaches the consistency you desire.
3. Transfer the cheese to a bowl and use it as you like.

SIMPLE FIRM VEGAN CHEESE

Ingredients:

- 1 cup cashew or soy milk, or 1 cup water + 1/3 cup soaked cashew
- 1 cup sweet potato, boiled
- 1 tbsp. soy sauce
- ½ tsp. cumin
- ½ tsp. paprika
- 1 tsp. salt
- 2 tbsp. nutritional yeast
- 2 cloves of garlic or 2 tsp. garlic powder
- Half a lemon's juice
- 2 ½ tbsp. agar-agar powder
- 1 cup cold water

Directions:

1. In a blender, combine all the ingredients except for the cold water and agar-agar powder. Blend them all until you get a smooth mixture.
2. Pour in the water in a small saucepan and add the agar-agar powder.
3. Mix the water and agar-agar powder well. Then, place the saucepan over low to medium heat.
4. Continue to mix until the agar-agar powder is completely dissolved. This will take about 5 minutes.
5. Add the agar-agar mixture in the blender. Blend it well with the pureed mixture.
6. Pour the mixture into your molds. You can use a ceramic bowl or silicon molds if they're available.
7. Place the cheese in the refrigerator for about 30 minutes or until the cheese has set.
8. Remove the cheese from the molds and serve.

QUICK VEGAN "GRATED" PARMESAN

Ingredients:

- ½ cup cashews, roasted
- 2 tbsp. nutritional yeast
- 2 tsp. garlic salt

Directions:

1. Place all the ingredients in a blender or food processor. Blend until the cashews are ground up.
2. Transfer the vegan parmesan into a spice shaker and use it on pasta and other dishes.

EASY CASHEW VEGAN CHEESE

Ingredients:

- ½ cup cashews, soaked in hot water for 1 hour and drained
- 3 tbsp. nutritional yeast
- 1 tbsp. cider vinegar or lemon juice
- 1 tbsp. maple syrup
- 1 ½ tsp. cornstarch
- 1 ½ tsp. agar-agar powder
- ½ tsp. salt
- Half a clove of garlic
- 1 cup water, divided into two ½ cups
- Preferred herbs and spices (optional)

Directions:

1. Mix all the ingredients in a blender or food processor except for the agar-agar powder and ½ cup water. Blend for about 1 minute or until you get a creamy texture.
2. Heat ½ cup water with agar-agar powder in a saucepan.
3. Add the blended mixture to the saucepan. Bring to a boil while stirring constantly.
4. Lightly brush your ceramic molds with oil. Then, pour the mixture into the molds.
5. Refrigerate the cheese for 2 hours or more.
6. Remove the cheese from the molds and serve.

VEGAN NUT CHEESE

Ingredients:

- ½ cup raw cashews, soaked for 3 hours and drained
- 1/3 cup water
- 1 tbsp. coconut oil
- 1 tsp apple cider vinegar
- Half a lemon's juice
- A pinch of salt

Directions:

1. In a blender, mix all the ingredients until smooth.
2. Line ramekins or other molds you have with plastic wrap.
3. Pour the cheese mixture into the molds.
4. Refrigerate for at least 2 hours or until the cheese is set. You may also freeze it if you want to speed things up.
5. Remove the cheese by turning the molds upside-down on a serving dish.
6. Remove the plastic wrap from the cheese and enjoy.

VEGAN AMERICAN CHEESE

Ingredients:

- 1 cup raw cashews, soaked and drained
- ¼ cup water
- ¼ cup lemon juice
- 1/3 cup nutritional yeast
- 1 red bell pepper, chopped
- 2 garlic cloves chopped
- 2 tbsp. red onion, chopped
- 1 tsp. yellow mustard
- 1 tsp. sea salt
- ½ cup cold water
- 4 tsp. agar-agar powder

Directions:

1. In a blender, mix all the ingredients except for the cold water and agar-agar powder. Leave the mixture in the blender.
2. In a saucepan, mix in cold water and agar-agar powder. Stir for 5 minutes over medium heat and bring it to a boil.
3. Once it starts to boil, adjust the heat to low and let it simmer while constantly whisking for 8 minutes.
4. Pour in the agar-agar mixture to the blender and process it again until everything is well-combined.
5. Pour the mixture into a lined rectangular baking pan that's at least ½ to an inch deep. Only fill halfway if you're using a ½-inch deep pan (quarter-filled for an inch-deep pan).
6. Refrigerate the cheese for at least 2 hours or until firm.
7. Cut the cheese into desired sizes and wrap each piece in waxed paper.

CHAPTER 5:

Soft & Fresh Vegan Cheeses

VEGAN COTTAGE CHEESE

Ingredients:
- 1 ½ cups firm tofu
- 1/3 cups silken tofu
- 1 tbsp. nutritional yeast
- 1 tsp. lemon juice
- 1 tsp. apple cider vinegar
- ½ tsp salt

Directions:
1. Use a blender to combine all the ingredients except for the firm tofu. Blend until you get a smooth mixture.
2. Pour the tofu mixture into a medium mixing bowl.
3. Break the firm tofu into small pieces and place it in the tofu mixture. Mix well and serve.

HERBS + GARLIC SOFT CHEESE

Ingredients:

- 2 cups cashews, soaked in cold water and refrigerated for 12 hours
- Zest from 1 medium lemon
- Juice from 2 medium lemons
- ¾ cup water
- 2 garlic cloves, minced (should yield 1 tbsp.)
- 2 tbsp. nutritional yeast
- 2 tbsp. olive oil
- ½ tsp. garlic powder
- ½ tsp. sea salt
- 2 tbsp. fresh dill, finely minced

Directions:

1. After soaking the cashews, drain and put them into a food processor.
2. Add all the other ingredients except for the fresh dill.
3. Start grinding and processing the ingredients until you get a smooth and creamy puree. You can taste it and add more ingredients until you get your desired flavor.
4. Place a colander or a mesh strainer over a mixing bowl. Then, lay down cheesecloth over the colander. Use about two layers.
5. Scoop the cheese and put it on the cheesecloth. Get all the corners of the cheesecloth and gather them, trapping the cheese inside. Gently twist the top to shape the cheese into a thick disc. Finally, secure it with one or two rubber bands.
6. Refrigerate the cheese and let it sit for about 6 to 12 hours. The longer you let it set, the better. This is to make sure that all the excess moisture is gone and that your cheese will hold its shape.
7. Unwrap the cheesecloth once ready to serve. Place the cheese on a serving dish. You can reshape it with your hands if needed.
8. Coat the cheese with chopped fresh dill and add more lemon zest if preferred.

VEGAN MOZZARELLA CHEESE

Ingredients:

- 1 cup cashews, soaked in cold water and refrigerated for at least 4 hours
- ¼ cup unsweetened soy milk
- 1 ¼ cup unsweetened dairy-free yogurt
- 3 1/3 tbsp. tapioca starch
- 2 tbsp. lemon juice
- 2 tbsp. refined coconut oil
- 2 tsp. nutritional yeast
- 1 ½ tsp. sea salt
- ¼ tsp. garlic powder
- 2 tsp. agar-agar powder
- ½ cup water

Directions:

1. In a medium container, create a brine. Fill the container halfway with some filtered water, 5-6 pieces of ice cubes, and a few pinches of sea salt.
2. Drain the cashews and put it inside a food processor or blender. Also add in the milk, yogurt, tapioca starch, lemon juice, coconut oil, nutritional yeast, sea salt, and garlic powder.
3. Process or blend them on high for about 2 minutes or until you get a smooth mixture.
4. Next, add the ½ cup of the filtered water to a medium-sized pot and place it over medium heat.
5. When the water starts to get hot, whisk in your agar-agar powder. Whisk it well and it should start looking like gel after 3 to 4 minutes.
6. Once this happens, pour the blended mixture in the pot. Continuously stir using a silicon spatula to avoid your cheese from burning or sticking.
7. After a few minutes, the cheese will become thicker. Once it becomes thick and stretchy, remove the pan from the heat.
8. Use an ice cream scooper to shape the mixture into balls. Drop each ball into the brine you made earlier.
9. After scooping all the mixture, cover the container and put it in the refrigerator. Keep the cheese refrigerated for at least 3 hours before serving.

VEGAN COTIJA CHEESE

Ingredients:

- 1 cup almonds, slivered
- 2 tsp. lemon juice
- 2 tsp. manzanilla olives brine
- A few pinches of salt

Directions:

1. Put the almonds, salt, lemon juice, and brine in a blender or food processor.

2. Blend or process the ingredients until they become crumbly in texture. This should take about 4-5 minutes. Taste and add more salt if needed. Also, don't over process the mixture to avoid getting almond butter instead.

3. Place the mixture into about 2 sheets of cheesecloth. Use these to squeeze out all the liquid from the cheese.

4. Secure the cheesecloth and put it in the fridge. Keep it refrigerated for about 24 hours.

5. Open the cheesecloth and transfer the cheese to a container. Crumble the cheese and use as desired.

TOFU HALLOUMI

Ingredients:

- 15 oz. (1 block) tofu, extra-firm
- ¼ cup lemon juice
- ¼ cup nutritional yeast
- 2 tbsp. olive oil
- ¾ tsp. sea salt

Directions:

1. Prepare a large tray lined with parchment paper before making the cheese.

2. Cut your tofu block crosswise into planks that are ½-inch thick. Cut each tofu slice again in half and transfer to the tray.

3. Whisk all the other ingredients together in a small mixing bowl. Make sure everything is well-blended and smooth.

4. Brush the tofu slices with the mixture. Coat all the sides of every slice evenly.

5. Cover the tray with plastic wrap and refrigerate for at least 2 hours. For better flavor, keep in the refrigerator for 12 hours.

6. Next, put a large skillet over medium-high heat.

7. When the pan becomes hot, place the tofu slices. Make sure that there are no tofu slices that overlap or are sticking to each other. You can do this 2 or 3 batches.

8. Cook each side for about 2-3 minutes or until the sides become golden-brown in color. Serve after cooking all the tofu slices.

VEGAN ALMOND RICOTTA

Ingredients:

- 1 ½ cups almonds, slivered, soaked for an hour in hot water
- ½ cup coconut cream
- 1 tbsp. nutritional yeast
- 1 tbsp. lemon juice
- 1 tbsp. white vinegar
- 1 tsp. salt
- ½ tsp. garlic powder

Directions:

1. Drain the almonds and put in a blender or food processor. Add in the other ingredients.
2. Blend the ingredients until you get a smooth and grainy texture.
3. Transfer the cheese to a serving dish or a container. Keep it stored in the refrigerator when not in use.

SWEETENED VEGAN MASCARPONE

Ingredients:

- 1 cup cashews, soaked for at least 2 hours or boiled for 10 minutes
- 2 tbsp. lemon juice
- 2 tbsp. coconut oil, melted
- 1 tbsp. agave
- 1 tbsp. apple cider vinegar
- 1 tbsp. water

Directions:

1. Drain the cashews making sure to remove as much liquid as possible. Put the cashews in a blender or food processor.
2. Add in all the other ingredients and blend or process. Stir in between the blending process. This will remove air bubbles, ensuring that you have a well-blended mixture.
3. Transfer the cashew mixture to a container or bowl lined with plastic wrap.
4. Cover the container and refrigerator for at least 8 hours or until the cheese becomes firm.
5. Remove the plastic wrap from the cheese and serve.

TWO-WAYS VEGAN FETA CHEESE

Ingredients:

- 12 oz. (350 g) tofu, extra-firm
- ½ cup refined coconut oil, melted
- 3 tbsp. lemon juice
- 2 tbsp. apple cider vinegar
- 1 tbsp. nutritional yeast
- 1 tsp. onion powder
- ½ tsp. garlic powder
- ¼ tsp. dill, dried
- 2 tsp. salt

Directions:

1. Put all the ingredients in a food processor. But, use only a teaspoon of salt.
2. Process the ingredients until you get a smooth texture. Taste the mixture and add in more salt if needed. Blend it again if you decide to add more salt.

Spreadable Feta

You can already serve the feta cheese after processing if you want a spreadable version of this cheese. You may also put the cheese in a container to refrigerate for a few hours. This will make the cheese a bit firmer and easier to put on a cheese board.

Firm and Crumbly Feta

If you want your feta cheese to be crumbly, firm, and shaped into cubes, follow these instructions:

a. Line a rectangular or square-shaped baking dish with parchment paper. Use a pan where you can spread the cheese to be 1- to 2-inch thick.

b. Spread the cheese into your baking dish. Push down evenly, making sure that there are no air pockets.

c. Cover and refrigerate the cheese for about 2 hours. This will prevent the coconut oil from separating from your cheese.

d. While waiting for the cheese, preheat your oven to 200°C or 400 °F.

e. Remove the cheese from the refrigerator and take off the cover. Bake it for 35 minutes.

f. Take it out from your oven. Don't worry if the cheese seems bubbly and soft. It will set once it's cooled down.

g. Let the cheese cool and place in the fridge for at least 4 hours.

h. Cut the cheese into cubes or crumble before serving or using.

VEGAN CASHEW BRIE

Ingredients:

- 2/3 cup raw cashews
- 4 oz. firm mochi blocks
- 1/5 cup (50 ml.) water
- 2 tbsp. nutritional yeast
- 1 tbsp. miso
- 1 tsp. apple cider vinegar
- A few pinches of salt

Directions:

1. Preheat your oven to 180°C or 350 °F.
2. In a saucepan, combine the mocha, cashews, and water. Cook over medium heat for about 10 minutes or until the mocha is sticky and melted.
3. Remove from the heat and add in the rest of the ingredients. Slightly mix them all together.
4. Make a smooth mixture using a food processor, blender, or a stick blender.
5. Transfer the cheese to a baking dish lined with parchment paper.
6. Bake the cheese for 20 minutes or until the cheese has slightly crusted on top.
7. Take it out of the oven and let it cool.
8. Cover the baking dish and refrigerate overnight before cutting and serving.

VEGAN QUESO BLANCO

Ingredients:

- 16 oz. tofu, extra-firm
- 4 cups salt water (water + 1 ½ tsp salt)
- ½ cup coconut oil, melted
- 2 tbsp. lemon juice
- 1 tbsp. nutritional yeast
- 2 tsp. apple cider vinegar
- 1 ½ tsp. salt
- ½ tsp. onion powder

Directions:

1. To make salt water, heat 4 cups of water and bring to a simmer. Then, add salt.

2. Break the tofu into chunks. Blanch the tofu chunks in the salted water for about 3 minutes. Drain the tofu and put in a blender.

3. Add all the other ingredients in the blender. Blend until you get a creamy and smooth texture.

4. Transfer the cheese to a container to let it cool. Once it's cooled, cover the container and refrigerate.

5. Keep the cheese in the fridge until it becomes crumbly and firm before serving. This may take several hours.

CHAPTER 6:

Hard and
Air-Dried Vegan Cheeses

CASHEW + MILLET AIR-DRIED CHEESE

Ingredients:

- 1 cup cashews, unroasted
- ¼ cup millet
- ½ cup water (for boiling millet)
- ½ cup water (for blending the cheese)
- 2 tbsp. coconut oil, melted
- 1-2 tbsp. miso
- 1 tbsp. non-dairy yogurt
- ½ tsp. sea salt
- Tapioca starch for shaping

Directions:

1. Cook the millet in a small pot with ½ cup water. Bring to a boil before covering. Simmer for 15 minutes or until the millet absorbs the water and becomes soft. Let it cool.

2. Place the cashew nuts in a bigger pot. Pour in water (covering the cashews) and boil for 10 minutes. Let it cool.

3. Add the millet, cashews, and all the other ingredients in a food processor or blender. Process the ingredients until you let a smooth mixture.

4. Transfer the cheese into a glass container. Ferment the cheese for 24 hours.

5. At this point, the cheese will have bubbles and will start to smell sour and yeasty. Stir the cheese to remove air bubbles. Place in the refrigerator overnight to become firm.

Fermenting and Shaping

1. Cover your counter or work area with plastic wrap and generously sprinkle on tapioca starch.

2. Take half of the cheese mixture onto the starch and sprinkle some more on top.

3. Using the plastic wrap, gently shape the cheese into a wheel.

4. Wrap the cheese wheel with parchment paper to keep its shape. Secure it with a string. Place the wrapped cheese wheel onto another piece of parchment paper.

5. Repeat steps 1-4 for the other half of the mixture.

Air-drying

1. Take a plastic container and place two layers of paper towels at the bottom.

2. Place the cheese with the additional parchment paper in the container. Cover the cheese wheels with two more layers of paper towel on top.

3. Don't cover the container with a lid. Place it in the refrigerator to start drying.

4. Leave the cheese for about 4-5 weeks. Turn the cheese wheels over every day. Sprinkle some salt on the first day you turn them.

5. Once the cheese becomes firm within 4-5 weeks of drying, remove the parchment paper wrapped around them. But, keep the parchment paper sheet under the cheese to keep them from sticking to the paper towel.

6. Replace the parchment paper sheets (not the ones wrapped around the cheese) and towels when they become very wet.

7. After 4-5 weeks, you can now taste and serve your cheese. You can also dry it longer if you want a stronger flavor.

VEGAN PROVOLONE CHEESE

Ingredients:

- 1 can or 13.5 oz. full-fat coconut milk
- ½ cup hot water
- 2 tbsp. agar-agar powder
- 1 tsp. + 1 tbsp. nutritional yeast
- 1 tsp. tapioca starch
- ¼ tsp. garlic powder
- ½ tsp. lemon juice

Directions:

1. Start preparing your molds by oiling them using spray oil or rubbing any unflavored oil. You can use any glass container as a mold.
2. Pour the coconut milk into a saucepan. Then, pour the hot water into the empty can of coconut milk. This will help get all the remaining coconut milk in the can so nothing is wasted. Pour the water into the saucepan.
3. Add all the other ingredients into the saucepan. Stir using a whisk.
4. Place the saucepan over medium heat and continue stirring until it boils.
5. Turn the heat down to low or until the mixture is barely boiling. Continue stirring for a few more minutes until it becomes very smooth.
6. When it's already smooth, quickly pour the mixture into your molds.
7. Let it cool without a lid at room temperature for 15 minutes. Then, put the containers inside the fridge. Refrigerate for about 2 hours or until the cheese is completely set.
8. Cut the cheese and use it as you wish.

VEGAN SWISS CHEESE

Ingredients:

- 1 can or 13.5 oz. full-fat coconut milk
- ½ cup warm
- 2 tbsp. agar-agar powder
- 2 tbsp. nutritional yeast
- 1 tbsp. tahini
- 2 tsp. lemon juice
- 2 tsp. apple cider vinegar
- 1 ¼ tsp. salt
- ½ tsp. onion powder

Directions:

1. Oil your chosen mold with some spray oil. Add some oiled wooden sticks into the mold to create the holes for your cheese.
2. Add all the ingredients in a saucepan and mix with a whisk.
3. Put the saucepan over medium heat and continue stirring until it boils.
4. Turn the heat down and continue to stir. Allow it to slowly boil for 6 minutes.
5. Pour the cheese mixture into the molds and let it sit for 15 minutes uncovered.
6. Refrigerate the cheese for about 3 hours still uncovered.
7. Remove the sticks and slice the cheese to serve.

GRATEABLE VEGAN PARMESAN

Ingredients:

- 1 cup dry raw cashews
- ½ tsp. sea salt
- 1 ¼ tsp. distilled white vinegar
- 2 ½ tsp. lemon juice
- A pinch of ground mustard

Directions:

1. Put the dry raw cashews inside a food processor. Process until you get a fine crumbled texture.
2. Add in the other ingredients and process until they're well-combined. It should have a smooth, dough-like consistency.
3. Put the mixture on some plastic wrap and begin to shape the cheese into a wheel.
4. Refrigerate the cheese overnight while covered in plastic wrap.
5. The cheese should be hard enough before grating or slicing.

SHAVED VEGAN BRAZIL NUT PARMESAN

Ingredients:

- 1 cup Brazil nuts
- ½ cup pine nuts
- ¼ cup nutritional yeast
- ½ cup sauerkraut juice
- 2 tbsp. miso
- 1 tsp. sea salt

Directions:

1. Soak the Brazil nuts in water. The water should be enough to cover all the nuts. Let it sit for 4 hours at room temperature.
2. Drain the nuts and transfer to a food processor or blender. Add in the rest of the ingredients and create a puree.
3. Once the mixture is smooth, transfer it to an airtight container. Let it sit for 2-3 days at room temperature.
4. On the second or third day, preheat the oven to 250°F or 121°C. Position the racks on the lower and upper thirds of your oven, giving ample space between them.
5. Line 2 large baking pans with parchment paper.
6. Spread the mixture on the lined baking pans using an offset spatula. Make sure to spread the mixture as thin as possible.
7. Place the baking pans inside the oven and bake the cheese for 30 minutes.
8. Interchange the positions of the baking pans from top to bottom and vice versa halfway through baking.
9. After 30 minutes or when the cheese turned golden brown and dry, remove them from the oven.
10. Let it sit on your counter to cool. Then, break the cheese into shards.
11. Keep them in an airtight container or serve immediately.

VEGAN GORGONZOLA

Ingredients:

- 7 oz. (half a block) tofu, water-packed and extra-firm
- ¼ cup organic coconut oil, refined and melted
- 2 tbsp. miso paste, mellow white
- 4 tsp. champagne vinegar
- 2 tsp. lemon juice
- 2 tsp. kosher salt or sea salt, fine
- ½ tsp. onion powder
- ¼ tsp. garlic powder
- 1/8 tsp. spirulina (blue-green algae powder)

Directions:

1. Line your mold with two layers of cheesecloth or plastic wrap. Use a glass, metal, or ceramic container for your mold. A plastic container that's BPA-free will also do. Make sure that it can hold 1 ½ cups of liquid.

2. Press and drain your tofu until no juices come out. Make it as dry as possible.

3. Crumble your tofu and transfer to a food processor. Add in all the ingredients except the algae powder. Process the ingredients until you get a very smooth mixture.

4. Transfer the mixture to a mixing bowl. Scatter the algae powder evenly by dotting it in different spots.

5. Fold the mixture. Do not stir. This will create a swirled blue-green pattern.

6. Transfer the cheese mixture to your prepared molds. Pack it tightly using a spoon and try to smoothen the surface as much as you can.

7. Cover the mold with the cheese with plastic wrap. Refrigerate for at least 8 hours. You can keep the mixture in the fridge longer to make sure the coconut oil becomes solid.

8. Once the cheese has set, remove it from the mold. You can now crumble or slice the cheese and serve.

VEGAN ALMOND GRUYÈRE

Ingredients:

- 1 cup almonds, raw and soaked at room temperature for 12 hours
- 1/8 cup wheat-based rejuvelac (more might be needed)
- A pinch of salt
- 1 heaping tsp. nutritional yeast
- 1 heaping tsp. light miso paste
- ½ tsp. salt (prepare more salt for sprinkling)

Directions:

1. Remove the almonds' skin. Discard the skin and rinse your skinned almonds.
2. In a blender, combine the skinned almonds with a pinch of salt and rejuvelac.
3. Blend the ingredients with your blender set at medium speed. As the almonds are breaking down, increase the speed of your blender until you get a very smooth mixture.
4. Place the mixture in a glass bowl. You can taste the mixture to make sure that it's as bland as raw almonds.
5. Cover the bowl and let the cheese ferment. Let it sit for about 2 days at room temperature.
6. Next, mix the fermented cheese with the miso paste, nutritional yeast, and salt in a bowl. Make sure to mix the ingredients well.
7. Line a bowl with 2-3 layers of cheesecloth. Then, transfer the mixture into the bowl and spread it out evenly. Make sure to smooth away any air pockets. Knocking the bowl on your counter also helps remove air pockets.
8. Wrap the cheese with the cheesecloth by gathering the edges and twisting them tightly. Secure it with a rubber band or twist tie.
9. Sprinkle some salt all around the cheesecloth's surface around your cheese ball. This will allow your cheese to last longer and avoid spoilage.

10. Place the wrapped cheese ball on a drying rack and let it sit for 1-3 days at room temperature. Expect that the liquid will be dripping from the cheese, so place a plate or bowl underneath to catch the drippings.

11. Once the cheese becomes quite solid and sharp, unwrap the cheese and shape it with your hands. You may also use a mold or a spatula when shaping the cheese.

12. Sprinkle salt all around the cheese and place it on the rack again. You'll need to air-dry the cheese for 2-4 days more. Remember to cover the cheese with one layer of clean cheesecloth to prevent it from catching dust.

13. You can already use, eat, or serve the cheese when it reaches your desired hardness and taste.

VEGAN CHEDDAR CHEESE

Ingredients:

- 2 cups cashews, raw
- 1 cup almond yogurt, plain and unsweetened
- ¾ cup water
- 2/3 cup nutritional yeast
- 1/3 cup miso, brown
- 1 ½ tsp. probiotic powder
- 1 ½ tsp. salt (prepare more for drying)
- 5 tbsp. tapioca starch
- 3 tbsp. agar-agar powder

Directions:

1. Prepare your raw cashews by soaking them overnight. Drain and rinse them when you're ready to make your cheese.

2. Put the cashews and the rest of the ingredients in a blender or food processor. But, leave out the tapioca starch and agar-agar powder. Process them until you get a thick, gold-yellow cream.

3. Transfer the mixture to a glass bowl and cover it with plastic wrap. Let it sit at room temperature for about 48 hours.

4. After 2 days, transfer the mixture to a saucepan. Add the agar-agar powder and tapioca flour. Whisk the mixture until all lumps disappear.

5. Heat the mixture at medium-low while continuing to stir and scraping the side of the saucepan. You may see some lumps forming during this step, but they should subside after 10 minutes. Once this happens, the cheese is ready.

6. Quickly spread the cheese mixture onto an 8x8-inch silicone mold or a cheesecloth-lined glass dish. Evenly spread and smoothen the top of your cheese.

7. Let it sit until it cools down to room temperature. Cover the mold and refrigerate the cheese for at least 4 hours or until the cheese firms up.

8. Once it's firmed, sprinkle a bit of salt on top of the cheese. Then, remove the cheese from the mold onto a cooling rack. Once on the rack, sprinkle some more salt along the cheese's edges.

9. Air-dry the cheese for 4 days, making sure that you don't crowd your cheese. Keep it away from other objects on your counter and cover it with one layer of cheesecloth.

10. After 4 days, flip the cheese over and air-dry for 4 days more.

11. Cut or slice the cheese before serving.

VEGAN TOMATO + HERBS CASHEW CHEESE

Ingredients:

- 3.5 oz. cashews, soaked and drained
- Two ½ cup water (for the agar-agar powder and for blending)
- 2 tbsp. nutritional yeast
- 1 tbsp. lemon juice
- 1 tbsp. tomato paste
- 1 tbsp. sun-dried tomatoes, chopped
- ½ tbsp. agar-agar powder
- 1 tsp. miso paste
- ½ tsp. basil
- ½ tsp. tomato
- Salt and pepper for seasoning according to your preference

Directions:

1. Combine the water and agar-agar powder in a small saucepan and place over low-medium heat. Bring to a boil while stirring constantly for about 3 minutes.

2. Transfer the thick jelly mixture to a blender and add in all the other ingredients except the sun-dried tomatoes. Blend them all together until you get a creamy mixture.

3. Season the mixture with salt and pepper. Taste the cheese and add more if needed.

4. Add in the sun-dried tomatoes. Don't overmix.

5. Pour the cheese mixture into your molds. You can use a silicon mold or a glass dish lined with plastic wrap.

6. Refrigerate the cheese for at least 2 hours or until firm.

7. Remove the cheese from the molds and transfer it to a cooling rack. Let it sit for a few hours or until it forms an outer rind.

8. Place the cheese onto a serving dish. Slice and serve.

VEGAN PISTACHIO CHEESE

Ingredients:

- 1 cup pistachios, shelled
- 1 ½ cups water, separated into two parts
- ½ cup nutritional yeast
- 1 tbsp. maple syrup
- 1 tbsp. apple cider vinegar
- 1 tbsp. agar-agar powder
- Half a lemon's juice
- 2 garlic cloves
- 2 pinches of salt

Directions:

1. Soak the pistachios overnight. Make sure the water covers the pistachios and add a pinch of salt.
2. In a blender, add one part of water and the other ingredients except for the agar-agar powder. Blend the ingredients together until smooth.
3. Put the other part of water and the agar-agar powder in a saucepan. Place the saucepan over medium-low heat and stir constantly for about 5 minutes. There shouldn't be any lumps in this mixture.
4. Remove the saucepan from the heat and pour in the pistachio mixture into the saucepan. Combine the two mixture together thoroughly.
5. Pour the cheese into your glass mold lined with plastic wrap. Then, place inside the fridge. Chill the cheese for 2 hours or until it is set.

CHAPTER 7:

Fermented and
Cultured Vegan Cheeses

BASIC CULTURED VEGAN CREAM CHEESE

Ingredients:

- 2 cups cashews, raw and soaked overnight
- 2 tbsp. vegan yogurt, plain and unsweetened
- ½ tsp sea salt
- Water (for blending)

Directions:

1. Drain the cashews and put in a food processor or blender. Process until it becomes a smooth mixture. You can add a tablespoon of water at a time to help the cashews become smooth.

2. If the mixture is warm because of the food processor, let it cool down first. Once it's cooled, add the salt and yogurt. Blend thoroughly.

3. Transfer the mixture to a glass container and cover. Let it sit at room temperature for about 24 hours. Then, taste the mixture. You can add more salt if you wish.

4. Let it sit for another 12 hours. You may also leave it longer if you want a stronger taste. If you're satisfied with the taste, then the cheese is ready to serve.

EASY CULTURED VEGAN CHEESE

Ingredients:

- 2 cups slivered almonds, blanched
- ½ cup water
- 2 tbsp. lemon juice
- 2 tbsp. nutritional yeast
- 1 tbsp. garlic, minced
- ½ tsp. sea salt
- Powder from 2 pcs. probiotic capsules
- 2 tbsp. fresh dill, finely minced
- Spice mix or ground pepper, freshly ground

Directions:

1. Put the slivered almonds in a blender. Add in the lemon juice, garlic, sea salt, and nutritional yeast. Blend until you get a smooth and creamy mixture. You may add a tablespoon of water at a time until you get a creamy texture.

2. Transfer the mixture to a bowl. Then, add in your probiotic capsule powder. Make sure to stir well using a plastic or wooden spoon only.

3. Lay 2 cheesecloth layers over a colander or mesh strainer. Scoop the mixture over the cheesecloth.

4. Gather the edges of the cheesecloth, twist the edges, and form the cheese into a disc. Secure the twisted cheesecloth with an elastic band.

5. Let it sit at room temperature for 48 hours. You can leave it longer for a tangier and firmer cheese.

6. After culturing the cheese, refrigerate for about 6 hours or until firmed and chilled.

7. Unwrap the cheese and remove the cheesecloth gently. Transfer it to a serving dish and reshape the cheese carefully.

8. Gently coat the cheese with minced dill and spice mix. Serve with vegetables, crackers, or anything you desire.

VEGAN CAMEMBERT

Ingredients:

- 4 cups cashews, soaked in water overnight
- Powder from 8 pcs. probiotic capsules
- 8 tbsp. water
- 1/8 tsp. liquid Penicillium candidum
- 2 tsp. sea salt

Directions:

1. Drain your cashews and transfer to a glass bowl. Pour boiling water onto the cashews and let sit for 2 minutes. Drain once more.

2. Put the cashews in a food processor. Add 8 tbsp. of water and blend for about 10 minutes or until you get a thick and smooth mixture.

3. Add the probiotic capsule powder and Penicillium candidum to the food processor. Blend for another 15 seconds.

4. The mixture should be thick, but smooth. If it's not smooth enough, add 1 tbsp. of water at a time to help it smooth out, but still retain its thickness.

5. Scoop the mixture to 2 cheesecloth layers in a colander, compress, and add a small heavy dish on top. Put the colander over a bowl to catch the drippings from the cheese. Let it drain for about 10 hours at room temperature.

6. Transfer the mixture to a bowl and refrigerate for 4 hours.

7. Once the cheese has firmed up, line a baking pan with parchment paper. Then, place three 4-inch springform pans on the baking pan. Line the sides of the pans with parchment paper.

8. Fill each springform pan with the mixture. Compress the cheese by pushing down on them.

9. Place the cheese in a room with a temperate between 11-13°C or 52-56°F. Cover the cheese to prevent it from drying out. Allow to age for 2 weeks. The aging process will fail if you place the cheese at a higher temperature.

10. For the first 3 days, flip the cheese carefully every day. On the 4th day, remove the cheese from the springform pans. Sprinkle salt on the cheese. Turn them over and sprinkle the remaining sides of the cheese.

11. Continue to flip them until the 7th day. On this day, the cheese should be firm enough to transfer to a bamboo mat.

12. Still, continue to flip the cheese every day for the remaining days. The molds should appear on days 5 to 7.

13. After two weeks, the cheese should be completely covered with a white rind. Wrap your cheese wheels with cheese paper or parchment paper. Refrigerate for about 2 days or more. The longer you keep them in the fridge, the stronger their taste will be.

14. After a few days in the fridge, your cheese is ready to serve.

VEGAN BLUE CHEESE

Ingredients:

- 3 cups cashews, raw and soaked overnight
- 2 tbsp. coconut oil
- Powder from 6 pcs. vegan probiotics capsule
- 1/8 tsp. or 1/16 tsp. powdered Penicillium roqueforti
- 5 tbsp. water
- Sea salt

Directions:

1. Drain the cashews and put in a glass bowl. Pour boiling water and let sit for 2 minutes before draining again.

2. Put the drained cashews in a food processor or blender. Add 5 tbsp. of water and the coconut oil. Blend it for 10 minutes or until you get a thick and smooth mixture.

3. Add the powder of your probiotics capsule and the Penicillium roqueforti in the blender. Blend for another 15 seconds. Your mixture should be smooth and thick.

4. Transfer the mixture to a glass bowl and cover with plastic wrap. Let it sit for 24 hours at room temperature to ferment. After this, refrigerate the cheese for 4 hours.

5. Line a baking pan with parchment paper and place small springform pans on the parchment paper. You may need 3 to 4 springform pans depending on the size you will use. Line the springform pans with parchment paper.

6. Fill each springform pan with your mixture and press down firmly.

7. Cover to keep humidity inside the pans for the cheese to age well. Place the baking pan with your cheese inside the fridge for 2 weeks.

8. On the 2nd day, sprinkle salt on top of the cheese and slightly rub it. Flip the cheese carefully and sprinkle more salt on the sides and top.

9. Continue to flip the cheese every day during the aging process. Your cheese should become moldy on the 7th day.

10. On the 2nd week or 14th day, scramble the cheese as if you're scrambling tofu in a glass bowl.

11. Use another set of springform pans lined with parchment paper. Fill them up with the scrambled cheese, but don't apply too much pressure.

12. Remove the cheese from the pans after shaping them. Place them on a lined baking pan and cover. Use a plastic box or anything that won't touch the cheese.

13. Refrigerate the cheese for another 3 weeks. Make sure to flip the cheese daily during this time.

14. The aging process would be a total of 5 weeks. After this, you'll get cheese with blue molds and it's ready to serve.

FERMENTED VEGAN CASHEW CHEESE

Ingredients:

- 2 cups cashews, soaked overnight
- Powder from 1 pc. probiotic capsule
- 1 tbsp. nutritional yeast
- 1 tbsp. lemon juice
- ¼ tsp. sea salt
- ¼-½ cup water

Directions:

1. Put the cashews in a food processor and process until smooth. Add a bit of water to help smoothen out the mixture. But, it should have a consistency similar to thick and creamy nut butter.
2. Add in the powder of the probiotic capsule and stir.
3. Lay 2 layers of cheesecloth on a strainer or colander. Transfer the cheese onto the cheesecloth.
4. Gather the edges of the cheesecloth and apply pressure on the cheese. You can use a heavy dish or a jar to apply more pressure. Let the cheese drain.
5. Leave the cheese to ferment for 24 hours at room temperature.
6. The cheese will have a tangy smell after 24 hours. But, it shouldn't have any discoloration or mold growth.
7. Stir in the sea salt, lemon juice, and nutritional yeast. Season it some more depending on your preference and serve, or use for other dishes.

CULTURED MISO CHEESE

Ingredients:

- 2 cups cashews, raw and unsalted
- 1 cup water
- 1 tbsp. miso paste, dark
- 3 tsp. sea salt, separate 1 tsp. and 2 tsp.
- ½ cup coconut oil

Directions:

1. Combine the water, cashews, and miso in a glass bowl. Stir until they're well-combined.

2. Cover the bowl and let it sit for 24 hours at room temperature.

3. Then, transfer the cultured cashews to a blender and add the coconut oil and 1 tsp. of sea salt. Blend the ingredients until you get a smooth and creamy mixture.

4. Pour the mixture into your mold lined with cheesecloth. You can use any glass container as a mold. Refrigerate the cheese for 4-6 hours until the cheese becomes firm.

5. Remove the firm cheese from your mold and the cheesecloth. Rub your remaining sea salt all over the cheese's surface gently.

6. Transfer the cheese onto a cooling wire rack and place it in a dark area. Let the cheese age for at least 7 days or longer. The longer you age the cheese, the stronger its taste will be.

7. Finally, transfer it to a serving dish or storage container.

VEGAN GOAT CHEESE

Ingredients:

- 1 cup cashews, raw and soaked overnight
- ½ cup macadamia nuts, raw and soaked overnight
- Powder from 1 pc. probiotic capsule
- ¼ cup water
- 1 tbsp. apple cider vinegar
- ½ tsp. sea salt
- Half a lemon's juice

Directions:

1. Blend all the ingredients together until you get a nice smooth mixture.
2. Transfer the mixture to a glass jar. Make sure it's sterilized. Cover it with some plastic wrap and secure with an elastic band.
3. Then, cover the jar again with a kitchen towel. Let it sit at room temperature overnight.
4. Remove the towel and plastic wrap to serve.

SOFT SUNFLOWER + PUMPKIN SEEDS VEGAN CHEESE

Ingredients:

- 1 cup sunflower seeds, soaked overnight
- 1 cup pumpkin seeds, soaked overnight
- 1 tsp. sea salt
- Powder from 2 pcs. probiotic capsules
- Water for blending

Directions:

1. Drain the sunflower and pumpkin seeds. Rinse them again. It's okay to soak the seeds together in one container.

2. Combine the seeds and all the other ingredients in a food processor. You can add a tablespoon of water at a time to help process the ingredients. Add as little water as possible. You should get a nice smooth mixture.

3. Pour the mixture into a glass jar and cover with a plastic mesh lid. Cover with a kitchen towel and place the jar on a dish.

4. Let the cheese sit at room temperature for 4 to 12 hours. Warmer room temperatures can speed up the fermentation process.

5. After half of the fermentation time, turn the jar upside-down. Let it tilt sideways to drain out the liquid whey.

6. The fermentation process is finished when the cheese has risen slightly in the glass jar. Avoid over-fermenting the cheese.

7. Put a lid on the jar and refrigerate to stop the cheese from fermenting.

8. After a few hours in the fridge, the cheese is ready to serve.

VEGAN TURMERIC PARMESAN CHEESE

Ingredients:

- 1 cup sunflower seeds, soaked overnight
- 1 cup pumpkin seeds, soaked overnight
- ½ cup sesame seeds, soaked overnight
- Powder from 2 pcs. probiotic capsules
- 1 tsp. turmeric
- 1 tsp. sea salt
- 1/8 cup lemon juice
- Water for blending

Directions:

1. You can soak the seeds together in one container. Drain the seeds and rinse them again.
2. Put the seeds and the rest of the ingredients in a food processor. Add a tablespoon of water at a time until you get a smooth mixture. Avoid adding too much water.
3. Transfer the mixture to a jar with a plastic mesh lid. Turn it upside-down and let the cheese culture for about 4 hours.
4. Then, spread the cheese onto baking pans lined with parchment paper. Spread it as thin as possible to speed up the drying process.
5. Leave it to dry for about 4 hours. When it's a bit dry, break the cheese into shards.
6. Leave it out again to dry some more. This may take a few days depending on how thick your cheese shards are.
7. Once the cheese shards are completely dry, place them in a food processor. Process until you get your desired texture.
8. Transfer the cheese in a spice shaker and use as you wish.

SUNFLOWER SEEDS + CASHEW VEGAN CREAM CHEESE

Ingredients:

- ½ cup cashews, soaked overnight
- ½ cup sunflower seeds, soaked overnight
- 1 cup Irish moss gel (you can make your own or buy online)
- Powder from 2 pcs. probiotic capsules
- 1 tbsp. dill weed
- 1 tsp. onion powder
- 1 tsp. sea salt
- ½ cup water

Directions:

1. Soak the cashews and seeds in separate containers. Drain the sunflower seeds, but not the cashews.
2. Place the cashews with the soaking water and all the ingredients in a food processor. Blend until you get a nice smooth mixture.
3. Transfer it to a jar and cover with a plastic mesh lid. Turn the jar upside-down and let the cheese sit for at least 4 hours.
4. Then, pour the cultured cheese into a glass mold. No need to oil or line the mold with plastic wrap. The cheese will easily slide out once set. Refrigerate until the cheese has firmed up.
5. Remove the cheese from the mold and place on a serving dish.

CHAPTER 8:

Melted Vegan Cheeses

EASY VEGAN MELTED CHEESE

Ingredients:

- 1 ½ cups water
- 1/3 cup vegetable oil
- ½ cup glutinous rice flour
- ½ cup chickpea flour
- 2 tbsp. nutritional yeast
- 1 tbsp. flax seeds, milled
- 1 tsp. salt
- 1/8 medium onion, minced
- 1 garlic clove, minced
- A pinch of black pepper, ground

Directions:

1. Combine water, rice flour, chickpea flour, flax seeds, and nutritional yeast in a saucepan. Once the flours and yeast are dissolved, add the garlic, onion, and oil.
2. Cook the mixture over low heat while continuing to stir. After about 10 minutes, it should have a consistency like that of melted cheese.
3. Remove from heat and season the cheese with salt and pepper.
4. Transfer to a serving dish and serve.

COCONUT MILK VEGAN CHEESE

Ingredients:

- 1 can full-fat coconut milk
- ¼ cup nutritional yeast
- 2 tbsp. tapioca starch
- 1 tbsp. agar-agar powder
- ½ tbsp. lemon juice
- ½ tsp. salt
- ½ tsp. garlic powder

Directions:

1. Mix in all the ingredients in a pot except for the tapioca starch. Place the pot over medium-low heat. Stir continuously and bring the mixture to a boil.
2. Gradually add the tapioca starch while stirring. Continue cooking for 5 minutes or until the cheese becomes stretchy and thick.
3. Pour the cheese into an oiled 4-inch springform pan. Let it sit to cool before refrigerating for about 2 hours or until the cheese is set.
4. Remove the cheese from the pan and transfer to a serving dish.

MELTY VEGAN MOZZARELLA

Ingredients:

- 1 cup water
- 1/2 cup cashews, raw
- 3 tbsp. + 2 tsp. tapioca starch
- 1 tbsp. nutritional yeast
- 1 tsp. apple cider vinegar
- ½ tsp. salt
- ¼ tsp. garlic powder

Directions:

1. Cook the cashews for about 10 minutes or until soft in a pot with water. Drain the cashews and rinse.

2. Add the softened cashews and all the other ingredients into a blender. Blend until you get a watery and smooth mixture.

3. Pour the mixture into a saucepan and cook over medium-high heat. Continuously stir for about 6 minutes.

4. Serve the cheese in the saucepan or transfer to a serving dish. This cheese is best served hot.

VEGAN QUESO

Ingredients:

- 1 ½ cups butternut squash, peeled, seeded, and cubed
- ½ cup cashews, raw
- ¼ cup vegan salsa
- 1 can (4.5 oz.) green chilies, diced
- 3-4 tbsp. water
- 2 tbsp. nutritional yeast
- 1 tbsp. lemon juice
- ½ tsp. salt
- ½ tsp. turmeric
- ½ tsp. paprika, smoked

Directions:

5. Cook the butternut squash and cashews in a pot. Make sure that they're covered in water. Cook until the squash is tender.

6. Drain the squash and cashews. Put them in a food processor and add in all the other ingredients except the water, salsa, and green chilies. Blend the ingredients while adding a tablespoon of water at a time. Add just enough water to make a smooth and fairly thick mixture.

7. Transfer the mixture to a pot and add in the green chilies and salsa. Put the pot over medium heat and slightly cook the queso until it becomes bubbly and thick.

8. Transfer the queso to a serving dish and serve immediately or let it cool down first.

MELTED VEGAN WHITE CHEESE

Ingredients:

- 1 ½ cups vegan milk
- ¼ cup nutritional yeast
- ¼ cup plain flour
- 2 tbsp. cornstarch
- 2 tbsp. tahini
- 2 tsp. lemon juice
- 1 tsp. onion powder
- ¾ tsp. salt
- ¼ tsp. garlic powder

Directions:

1. Blend all the ingredients in a food processor or blender until you get a smooth mixture.
2. Pour the mixture into a saucepan. Heat and cook the cheese over medium-high. Stir constantly using a whisk until smooth and thick.
3. Transfer it to a serving dish and serve hot.

CHAPTER 9:

Nut-free Cheeses

VEGAN SESAME CHEESE

Ingredients:

- ½ cup sesame seeds, un-hulled
- 1/8 cup nutritional yeast
- 1 cup water
- 1 tbsp. agar-agar powder
- 1 tbsp. apple cider vinegar
- ¼ tsp salt

Directions:

1. Put the sesame seeds, salt, and nutritional yeast in a food processor. Grind until you get a flour texture.

2. In a saucepan, simmer the water and agar-agar powder over medium-low heat for 5 minutes. Remove the saucepan from the heat and let it cool for 5 minutes.

3. Pour the agar-agar mixture to the food processor. Blend them together until you get a smooth mixture.

4. Line a glass bowl with plastic wrap. Pour the cheese mixture in the bowl, cover, and put in the refrigerator.

5. When the cheese becomes firm, remove from the glass bowl. Peel away the plastic wrap and put the cheese in a serving dish.

NUT-FREE VEGAN GRUYÈRE

Ingredients:

- 2 tbsp. nutritional yeast
- 2 tbsp. tahini paste
- 2 tbsp. apple cider vinegar
- 2 tbsp. oats
- 4 tsp. cornstarch
- 1 tsp. onion powder
- 1 tsp. garlic powder
- ¼ tsp. salt
- 1 cup water

Directions:

1. In a food processor, combine and process all the ingredients until you get a smooth mixture.

2. Transfer the mixture to a saucepan. Cook the cheese over medium heat and continuously stir. Continue to cook the cheese for 5 minutes or until it becomes thick.

3. Turn off the heat and stir for another 2 minutes. Remove the saucepan from the stove and allow it to cool.

4. You can now use it for other recipes or serve as it is.

MARINATED TOFU VEGAN FETA CHEESE

Ingredients:

- 115 oz. tofu, extra-firm
- 1/3 cup olive oil
- 1 tbsp. dried tomatoes
- 2 tsp. Dijon mustard
- 1 tsp. mixed peppercorns
- 1 tsp. salt
- 1 tsp. rosemary, dried or fresh
- ½ tsp. garlic powder
- ½ tsp. red pepper flakes
- 2 bay leaves
- 4 sprigs of thyme
- 1 lemon wedge
- A few fresh mint leaves

Directions:

1. Cube the tofu. In an airtight jar, combine the tofu and all the ingredients.
2. Refrigerate for at least 3 days.
3. Take out the jar after 3 days. Pour the contents of the jar in a skillet. Sauté over medium-high heat for 7 minutes.
4. Return the sautéed cheese in the jar together with the liquid and herbs. You can also transfer it to a serving dish and serve.

VEGAN PIMENTO CHEESE

Ingredients:

- 1 can (114 oz.) chickpeas
- 1 jar (14 oz.) sliced pimentos
- ½ cup vegan mayonnaise
- 2 tbsp. nutritional yeast
- Salt and pepper for seasoning

Directions:

1. Drain the pimentos and chickpeas and discard the liquid.
2. Put all the ingredients in a food processor. Process until you get a smooth, creamy texture. Taste the cheese and season with salt and pepper if needed.
3. Transfer the cheese to a serving dish or in a glass jar and serve.

CHICKPEA FLOUR VEGAN CHEDDAR CHEESE

Ingredients:

- 1 cup chickpea flour
- 2 ¼ cups water (1 cup and 1 ¼ cups separated)
- ½ cup nutritional yeast
- 2 tbsp. cider vinegar
- 2 tbsp. tahini
- 1 tbsp. paprika, smoked or sweet
- 1 tbsp. yellow mustard
- 1 tsp. onion powder
- ¾ tsp. sea salt, fine

Directions:

1. Whisk the paprika, salt, onion powder, flour, and nutritional yeast in a medium mixing bowl.
2. Gradually add 1 cup of water while whisking. Then, whisk in the vinegar and mustard.
3. Put the remaining water in a saucepan and bring to a boil. Set the heat to the lowest setting possible and whisk in the tahini and chickpea mixture. Continue to whisk and cook for 7 minutes. You should have a very thick mixture by this time.
4. Transfer the mixture immediately to a 9x5-inch loaf pan. Smooth the top.
5. Let the cheese cool at room temperature. Then, loosely cover the pan and refrigerate for about 2 hours or until the cheese is very firm.
6. Drain any liquid that the cheese will release. Transfer it to a cutting board. Cut, slice, cube, or shred the cheese before serving.

CHAPTER 10:

How to make
the Ultimate Vegan Cheese Board

After making a lot of vegan cheeses, it's sure that you'd want to show them off to friends and family. The best way to serve your homemade vegan cheese is by creating a cheese board. It'll look classy and expensive, but it's quite easy to make.

Here are the things to keep in mind when making the ultimate cheese board for your vegan cheeses:

- The most important thing is the **wooden board**. This will hold the cheeses and other food items. Remember that the larger the board, the harder it will be to fill up because you'll need a lot of food for it.

- You can get an expensive slate board or a cheaper wooden cutting board. If you're using a cutting board, make sure it's new and only used to make a cheese board. You won't want to ruin your cheese board with unwanted smells or stains.

- Serve a *variety of cheeses* on your cheese board, allowing your guests to choose depending on what they prefer. Have a variety of hard and soft cheeses as well as cheese sauces.

- Choosing **food items** is the next thing you'll have to think about. You'll need savory items, sweet items, spreads (not including your vegan cheese spread), and bases. You'll need to have at least 2-3 kinds of each.

    a. Savory items include vegan deli meats and pickled vegetables.

    b. Sweet items are fruits. They can be dried or fresh. It's best to cut fresh fruits them into thin slices.

    c. Examples of spreads you can use are jams, mustard, pâtés, and chutneys. Include a savory and a sweet spread on your board.

    d. Bases are food items that will accentuate the taste of your cheeses. They usually have mild tastes to pair with the other items on your board. Some examples of bases are crackers, baguette, and bagel chips.

- Once you've decided on the food items to put on your board, it's time to decorate! You can arrange your cheese board any way you like. But, keep in mind to not group food items together. Scatter your savory items, sweet items, bases, and spreads across the cheese board.

The highlight would be your cheeses, so you'd also need to position them around the board. Once you've arranged everything in place, fill in the spaces with some nuts and fresh sprigs of rosemary.

CHAPTER 11:

Keep Your Vegan Cheese Journal

It's easy to find vegan cheeses anywhere nowadays. But, finding the best ones out there can be a struggle for many cheese lovers and enthusiasts. That's why you should keep a vegan cheeses journal.

A *cheese journal* is used to record notes about the different cheeses you've tried. It's an essential tool, especially for people who make homemade vegan cheese.

There are some ready-made cheese journals available in the market. They already have a template for each page so all you have to do is fill them up.

But, you can also make your own personalized cheese journal if you have time to spare. A common cheese journal would have these information categories:

- Name of cheese
- Origin and producer
- Type of milk
- Cheese's style
- Cheese's age
- Pasteurized or raw
- Aroma and flavor description
- Texture description

These categories are for dairy cheeses. So as a vegan cheese consumer, it's best to make your own. If you'll use this journal for the vegan cheeses you'll make at home, it can double as a recipe book as well.

Making a vegan cheese journal will help you remember what cheeses you liked and the recipes you want to do again. It'll also help you identify the areas you have to improve on to make your cheeses better.

CONCLUSION

I'd like to thank you and congratulate you for transiting my lines from start to finish.

I hope this book was able to help you create the different types of vegan cheeses that you've been dreaming of. With these easy-to-follow recipes and tips, you'll surely enjoy making vegan cheeses all the time.

The next step is to continue learning and exploring the different aspects of vegan cheese making. Who knows? You might be able to make your own recipe in the future.

I wish you the best of luck!

25024935R00047

Printed in Great Britain
by Amazon